Ladies Lost in Wonder:

A Literary Work Composed in 2020

GIORGIO ARMATI

AuthorHouse™ UK
1663 Liberty Drive
Bloomington, IN 47403 USA
www.authorhouse.co.uk
UK TFN: 0800 0148641 (Toll Free inside the UK)
UK Local: 02036 956322 (+44 20 3695 6322 from outside the UK)

Because of the dynamic nature of the Internet, any web addresses or links contained in this book may have changed
since publication and may no longer be valid. The views expressed in this work are solely those of the author and do not
necessarily reflect the views of the publisher, and the publisher hereby disclaims any responsibility for them.

Any people depicted in stock imagery provided by Getty Images are models,
and such images are being used for illustrative purposes only.
Certain stock imagery © Getty Images.

This book is printed on acid-free paper.

ISBN: 978-1-6655-8822-5 (sc)
ISBN: 978-1-6655-8823-2 (e)

Print information available on the last page.

Published by AuthorHouse 04/09/2021

authorHOUSE®

Ladies Lost in Wonder:

A Literary Work Composed in 2020

Giorgio Armati

Book 1

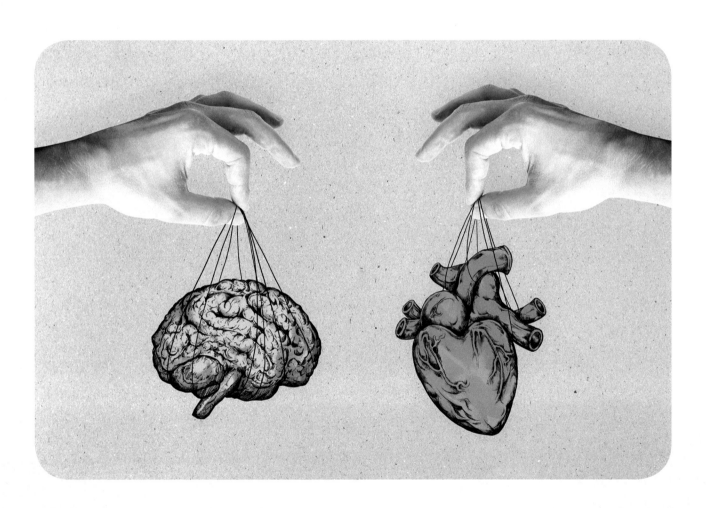

Preface

I tried to reevaluate and discover different emotional statuses that are perhaps new in this year 2020 due to all the changes that are taking place around the world. It seems we sometimes forget to ask questions or face off about what can make everyone vulnerable or strong as they confront the seemingly impossible way in which life presents itself.

Social isolation and restrictions on social life and relations have given many of us—at least for me—time to analyse such topics. I wanted to collect my thoughts and observations in poetry form, especially from what seems to be the point of view of women.

The Given Path

It's not so sure
that some matters
pull out an outcome willingly accepted.

On the verge of collapse,
a mind tends to strengthen the body
to march.

Directions are man-made;
the real path that everyone must attend
is given.

What Is Love?

Love is a service
when due is paid with solitude.

Love is an insolent act also,
which has no mercy.

A man can love what desires,
a woman instead loves what
that invisible string
is attached to.

So if someone should ask,
my string is attached to a purpose or path,
as many with few joys
and many struggles.

To live again a determinate moment
seems a foolish desire; indeed, who can see all those strings?

The Love of a Blind

Who is blind
yet can see
love is not given
because forbidden?

Because cannot give away
what belongs to someone else.

Some attachments
could be delusions for him or her
if that force* wanted not to be deceived,
in order not to make suffer their hearts.

How can a heart learn without
feeling detachment or pain?

Do you blame, dear reader,
those fears? Or acceptance can come in
as the will to seek
that peace that can let a love, or lovers,
sleep at night.

And so, I'm blind
yet still can see and force not
to see or find
if thy bound was made only to be found.

Note: *Force: intended as connection.

The Shape of Shadows

One night saw clearly myself

One lady running away from herself.

Are those shadows perilous advisors,
or nowadays do such minds go to visit
a twisted affection inside an illusion?
Why do those shadows bring oneself on such a voyage?

One night seeing
my dim figure that was standing close to the bed,
comprehension came
in absence of light;
there is not an I, you, he, she, we, or them.

At least the end or the beginning
of an opaque emotion.

The Scent of a Teacher

Walking in a dream,
I was enjoying the beauty of nature
reassembled with collective memories.

Met a woman in a hurry;
she presented herself as a teacher,
but I didn't listen to her cry.

Something was lost and hadn't been found.
Departed to search for what was lost.
Was it a person, an object, or what else?

Running to where she gently pointed,
a scent came while the surroundings
were changing from forest to desert,
from sea to mountain.

Was such scent of those places
what she needed to find
in one's other dream?

Note: Elaboration of a lucid dream where I found myself looking for something with this woman who said she was a teacher.

The Crow's Song

Duel of souls,
portrait of damaged animus,
a crow observes his way from the sky.

Looks beyond human eyes.
Looks where we don't dare.
Sometimes goes where
mystical appearance
is shattered between worlds.

He never feels alone,
flies where he has to be,
doesn't ask,
doesn't answer.
Indeed, his appearance
makes me tremble when he does caw.
Likes to say,

'I'm a crow, and I've witnessed things.'

Bending Thy Heart

Oblivion of emotions,
where people more able have been
dared not if their hearts cannot hold.

As one wonders, bending my own,
stretching thy will,
the only thing left behind,

a shredded breath
and a heartbeat
made of broken rock.

The Mind in a Soul (or Anima)

Where there was darkness,
the thought of human
was born surrounded.
The wounds of an anima,
as many burn until flaring itself.
The devourer begins to fear
to become ash.

A soul without purpose,
only energy that overlaps
against the titans
for a minute with a piece of destiny.

Note: The noun "devourer" is metaphor for a mind that lose stability and falls
into an unconscious status where primordial emotion or instinct prevails. For

example, in situations that are hard to control, if there is not emotional support or a guide, those primordial emotions tend to guide people in a dangerous position or unexplored status of mind, where the reality observed can be distorted by an excess of overviewing and acceptance of what can be impossible can actually be a reality.

Confrontation of Hearts

Which desire has won.
is unconquered?
The heart's shout remains unshaken
even when it hurts.

The guide and the guided,
not by the wish of glory,
tried to conquer
an antique grave.*

One heart went on the edge;
the other awaits its salvation.
Which heart belongs to whom?

Note: Antique grave: There is a story in one of Carl Gustav Jung's book where a king went to open the grave of a woman. Symbolically, from that came out a black horse that was hard to catch at first. This represents the idea that it can be difficult to adapt old values to the modern era. It can be hard to adjust to the new, fast, and sometimes unconscious way to reconsider life itself nowadays.

What's the Meaning of the Word "End"?

Some walk into this word
with harsh eyes,
tasting probably
the conquest of memories
and contorted pleasure,
having to stand where cold reigns.

Their silent screams have left
a print in history, yet
they desire not to be remembered.
It seems the only thing
for them was walking

into the change that such a word
can complain.

This sound does not reassemble anger or joy,
just the need to be heard.

Heart's Hidden Fear (Part 1)

The past, running through the mist of times
old and new, disappears in the trick of ill foot.
Why hide the form of an idea
if you or what else doesn't confront
into a symbolic vessel?

The past needed to dissolve
such lack of spirit if trade
or not her own freedom.
Why look for an old servant?

Felt her connected fears,
saw drawing a flower,
how discovering herself took a vow of commitment,
the renounce to grip a gift of power,
to learn again to listen to oneself or herself.

Renounce: This was her fear that became strength.

Heart Hidden Fear (Part 2)

Present a unity I put aside for a while
to listen to a teaching of man, such as,
we're all one.

So give off my own fears
for a misunderstanding
those mutated in a moment of bright consciousness.

Now, in this static present,
share this small knowledge of mine
as required patience, some women showed,
regarding my own lack.

Because was not a man needed
but a slow walk toward a direction
of hardship.

Can it be a direction or multitude of directions
toward uncertainty, a hidden fear of an old heart?
Or just the way to make possible for others to see
all those ways?

Which answer compels the readers?

The Darkness in the Night

All seems to be transitory,
a lost beat.

Walking into this shell,
someone grasps her breath
to listen to those little jumps

crafted, heartbeat of thy persona.
With closed eyes, she borrowed
and exchanged an unbounded pulse.

Was worthy for that traveller
searching into the darkness of nights
a piece doesn't belong if just to one,
was that small measure of peace enough to shake a whole?

Crossing the Hatch

Saw the fragments
of scattered minds,
rented those colours
while they were observing the scent.

If now you are here or there,
what divides two lovers from not being
pleasant to an idea
that is not a remedy?

So disclose the hatch.
An old brother made a question
about the reader, and the answer seems still hidden.

What's the real need
before a crow's song
will bring myself to sleep?

Note: Hatch in this context means to disclose something, an emotion or status about feelings, that sometimes puts a mind in sleepy mode. Everyone knows how an emotion can make a mind insecure or perhaps go into limbo.

Riddle

I'm the chain that imprison minds, not made of steel.
Indeed, the cold grip is perceived with little discord. What has been imprisoned if not a cursory emotion that doesn't know shelter
in predators' eyes. Which feeling is so fleeting for who reads?

Number 9

Huntress headache, nine times of missing a hunt.
Hold her mark of a conclave promise,
touching thy strings of a deluded reality.
Nine lives as a cat thriving to reach a self
went beyond her comprehension.

Heart Hidden Fears (Part 3)

Future, a derisory state
of commitment where chaos retreats,
travelling to shake people's hearts.

Nature gives a gift of premature minds
and cruel-sized those ungifted
for whom challenge thy supremacy.

A nature that does not nurse artificial minds,
looking for a consciousness that a woman
would put on her scale with some fears and questions.

So which man walks free
along with defeat or victory on those long journeys ahead?
Embrace all as gifts for one that should moet
along the road.

Decoy

From where comes their needs?
Enslavement of passions,
no regards even if a purpose has been given.

Sky cries sometimes
for unwritten story.
Why should add some more sweet tears out of
the cloudy blue?

Decoy of mindful project,
plan on my own.
Where is this word some whisper in my head?

A reservoir before met the order,
so thus what has been done,
a consideration for her deeds.

It is something ... or it is not.

The Unspoken Word

Wondering in this heart,
showing a hidden beat,
what should say a man
with unspoken words?

A man doesn't pledge or take
what doesn't belong to him.
Some pages will stay unwritten
because there is no duty in writing
a truth that is peril for unstable emotions.

A crow speaking in the ears of a young lady wonders,
Shall not whom wonder
open her young heart unless if asked
gently?

Note: Experience deduces from hopes and desires of young women to whom I have spoken a few times, trying to give my best advice.

Between the Bird and Worm

Which prey is constantly
undertaken if not in the will of an act?
A bird walks from side to side of a garden.

The worm quietly slides away
between being a bite
or being where belongs,
digging into the fissure of earth.

Leaving empty space
for those seeds that fall
from trees, unexpected, involuntary.

The Edge of Woman

Claiming a dance
with dirty pawns
can leave signs of despair
if pleasure has not reached all darkened corners.

What does she need to prove
for herself or to herself,
worthy existence or a decent living?

Let me see, or letting the reader think,
there is no feeling that proves
to be existed.
Only a collection of small deeds
when recalled can give relief.

Maybe she is looking for relief
from herself.

The Sound of a Cut

Cutting its own roots
must have a purpose.
The sound of an action
when meaning goes inside
could render that freedom
for those who look
abidance from such bound.*

Am I awake again?
Under which strings?
Which emotions does someone need to rediscover?

Probably the only aim was to re-establish
that light in those hearts.
The price asked from a regular man this time
is the freedom of servitude.
Indeed, that line is not mine affair to overcome.

Note: Abidance from such bound: In my experience, I've been in to the point, as have many, of having to learn to let things go, even when those things have returned multiple times. It is a strange feeling when sometimes everyone can be put in a threatening situation to deal with old bindings that are hard to untie. They present themselves in different situations but with the same aims to build again something that had expired.

For myself, it was essential to understand why this search was for many just a disconnection from a moral relativism that even if it showed the real essence of such action, didn't grow up in a feeling of acceptance.

The Black Heart

No crossing hatch?
Safety a nice feeling.
What mind is not yours
hold thy step.

A black heart* does not impose conditions
on what is not still.
Indicate a path
that fear imprisons a person.
Fear of not feeling?
Fear of not reaching perfection?

Understand the meaning of those who are unbound
is just as simple as reading a misguided symbol.

This moment a woman is looking for,
only to slide away from others.
Close a door and open another,
finding that drive and leaving all unconquered.

Which steps are needed?
Flip this mind as the wind does.
Let move those unmovable steps.

What a black heart can need
is a missing deep breath
into cut roots with no memories as chains.

Note: Our culture has defined 'black heart' as those who seem without regard toward feeling, evil, or corrupt. In part this is true. But this is due to the fact that the experience of diversity can bring different visions of a story or a life to those who listen or read such sharing moments. Sometimes it's needed to become little black-hearted only to have time to spend with oneself. What I recollect as memories, some women, and some men do in different proportions, choose to leave some stories with no results or clarifying moments to relieve or at least update some kind of knowledge regarding human relationships.

The Grape and the Fox

It was said that a fox
couldn't reach a grape,
a fable of misguidance
for those who haven't danced.

So much turbulence
in keeping what does not belong
to a creative hand,
futile rage of a heart that has everything.

What is a luxury drink
without a cold dish?
All served—all in or all out—
who dare to win the price full of solitude.

What has been done
that concerns the price of what is undone?
Why not taste your wine
from the lips of others?
'It seems too inappropriate,' the fox spoke
after leaving the grape that he reached.

Black Eyes

Was a lady calm but disappointed
no mirror in the cave
of a black heart?
Can a mirror reflect a purposed desire
or just distort the image of it?

What could see a lady
through it?
Reflections of past, present, or future?
Could she have seen her eyes
in a stranger?

Finding an unexpected bound,
how many questions
she couldn't answer.

Immerging herself into a mist
was a moment of high and low,
hearing her beat between the throat and the chest.
She left her beat being stolen.

The Lack of Acceptance

Doesn't show its face;
brings silent words to his lips,
and in a moment is gone.

A force that deceives
forced to a corner
by the logos of creation.

Vague spirits chained
with no acceptance learned,

and make them wander
weightless in this life.

Everyone looks for what is missing
of their own in others.
Someone looks to have, to possess,
or just having something to look at.

What's the difference in being incomplete
or unlikely complete?
Acceptance of own incompleteness.

Note: Sometimes in human relations what one has been looking for is adventure, drama, or something else. The point is, in my experience, acceptance of understanding that there is always something incomplete about the self should be regarded as key to opening up to others. Obviously, with time those who walk an unconventional path develop a different way to be complete, or at least to detach from the mind that someone else should complete them in this life.

Memories of a Mother

For those will see
too late
the love of their mothers ...

Those women should not bow
their heads to a stranger.

But let heart's stranger
bow to their strength

until those children
can open own eyes
in front of such emotion.

Book 2

Preface

I tried to give readers a sense of how feeling and human relations work out. I put myself in a mode to follow a condition in which, even if the negative counterpart of caring is known, loving has been not totally revealed. I have tried to use simple words to describe various circumstances and moments of defiance in which there is understanding that perfection doesn't exist in a bond between men and women. An exception is in the recognition that the turmoil needs to be overcome before having the pleasure to live those moments which define human persona.

The Pleasure of Wind

Why try to catch a pleasure
that comes by itself?
Greedy hands
search for a dawn of revelation.

Forced destiny
that has broken;
hybrids that cannot be conquered
with force or mischievous deeds.

So all those resolutions
go away with the cold and chilly wind,
which will change that unpersuasive way
and make the madness pretend
to chain an unmovable force.

Wish It Will Never Stop Raining

Lodging through the world,
guided by sight maybe,
the anima come back from such rapture.

There was a gentle woman
who shared a moment of wonder,
finding in it a familiar farewell, a common vision of life.

Sometimes seems not enough.
Leaving enough space inside,
A wish for her that she gave lodging

on rainy days with no minds.
Water stopping its fall
while she walks inside.

Has she found purpose before or after
the day was left with a memory of small gifts?

Note: Maybe once or a few times in a lifetime, a friendship is unveiled beyond the normal life, a connection that in some way is not chosen or that one is even conscious of. In that moment, such things seem not to be permitted in social contests, so they are still a little incomprehensible. Believe that everyone has been in that situation.

It seems that the only thing to do is avoid the wild game around and leave a gift just to remind that person there was at least one person who understood her or his point of view.

The Fall of Jackal

So sweet, so bitter,
example of disguise.
Where are your power and belief
in a love that never vanishes?

Stolen pockets, stolen memories
that jackal has all back up;
it is an expensive affair
or a need to carry on such a life for mere supremacy.

Lost children with painted hands,
no escape, no lie to hide the real colour of an essence.
All deeds counted for every drop
of mischief, intolerance
for such preaching.

Note: I used the word "jackal" in the title because love sometimes changes even the best person and almost mutates perception of our cognitive capacity.

Love, if not accepted or is used as a manipulative tool, can hurt those who use it and those who are under such a condition. So, as one of a strong emotions in human repertory, it is still underrated due the high consciousness that comes with aging. So when I use the line, 'lost children with painted hands', I imagine a child who tries to discover the essence of such feeling for which every adult has a corrosive or even burning status that, at its passage, doesn't leave positive changes if they do not have the necessary strength to living such moments with weightless minds.

A Lost Heart

Two hearts conflicting with each other
for a small pleasure of peace.
Those have seen decay
into a black heart will to pursue
the sky.

Those who found or are destined to be
such hearts are servants
almost lost in an endless wonder.

Thy bones would like to rest
in such arms, which would disclose first
the one who feeds the desire,
or one who just walks undisturbed
by indiscrete eyes.

Maybe it's a moment that cannot
be bought or conquered.
There are no compliments in a lost wonder,
just a braze alive in a shell,
where an essence is resting
only for that moment.

Note: To be clear, there is nothing wrong with wonder, but accepting and letting
go are part of this life. And in that search, who doesn't get lost?

The Needle That Stings

The sweetest moment in which a man or a woman
awaken for each other,
what aim to hold a cold hand
that cannot keep a love,
so talked some minds with open but blind eyes?

So thus walk
in the dark valley of boulevard dreams.
A lady or a sir in some stage
doesn't look at a rented sin.

Educating for a value that builds heroes
or just common sense
to perceive a needle that stings.
Who could push it out?

Needle of remembrance—
Have any readers ever known that sensation?
A sensation that seems a question

to be part of something or someone,
without knowing a mind can turn a heart
in stone.

Healing is not easy.
Sometimes a good justification
to find a judge that can weigh
those hearts and remove such needles.

Policing Love

Unexplored paths and yet strangely known,
a lady walks with a crow's song.
reminding that a regret doesn't come
to punish unclaimed deeds.

Followed partners or ghosts
in safety games,
No escalation is sold away
in this mist.

Can a policy be added to a connection
of caring? How can love be given in return?
Blue lights, rushing lady,
eyes that cross, and a moment
to understand that they are not made for each other.
Regret of such knowledge in growing age.

Love seems an artist on its own
that fools even the best crafter.
Cold bed with no lust to consume,
is there a mirror to capture again
such a portrait?

Note: In this strange modern age, while looking to amplify and make stronger
connections, nature seems willing to impose or at least remind us that some
relationships are not made by our own wills or choices. Picturing someone's image
in a mirror seems not enough to recognise the change that some people bring to
our lives.

Resting One Day

If it was permitted to rest with no conquest or glory,
marching alone through the mist
as many, to wonder where the inner voice
spoken of sight—

even when someone else beyond the sky
claims what belongs to none except one—

this corrupted mind of mine
requires to rest
in not chosen arms
or still battle itself.

Which words proclaim from fraud, villain,
hero, transform a creature
to hold at bay others' wonders
from unexplored land of the unconscious?

Have not found, visited
a lost corner of paradise, or at least
the courage of such eyes
that have seen where those belong.

Are those perceptions possible
to fall asleep, or even if
maybe it is all a lucid dream?

Synchronicity

Lovers, sailing on high water,
looking for answers in different places,
bounding what cannot be bound
by its own will.

Have those learn to focus
on intention, without letting burn
or lose sense synchronicity in human connection,
sound like a burden sometimes.

Mirroring reality,
confronting a pain, does such as
belongs to the writer or to one reader.

Indeed, from reality of a storm there is always a shelter.
But from the reality of words, futile is trying
to escape because such letters will be heard
by others' lips.

Synchronicity: A dream can be strong,
such as a wish or a desire.
What matters the difference if not to admire
thy beauty such words impress in human will?

Search the synchronicity of one's desire or wish or need,
or the strength to compel them in one's hand.

Note: Reader, which synchronicity are you looking for?

The Golden Needle

In the chess of life,
strategy is not enough
to understand an unmovable force.
Even if conquered, what makes such power
so anchored to one point?

Even the free will
given by the extreme
to learn the strength needed to let it go,
where is the solution in comparing
those forces?

The gift to envision thy differences
is a needle hidden in millions or more uncountable.
Will thy conquest for such a gift or revelation
satisfy your search?

Note: Understanding life or trying to hack its meaning has its pro and cons, so when such a search for meaning pops up in one's life, independent from which contest, arguing the basic topic from where one envisions an adequate perspective are the same, such as free will as a conquering ability or a given one; immovable force, static ideas that seem built inside humans for which every attempt to exploit those concepts brings one back to the starting point of questioning such ideas or at least understanding how this happens. It is then repeated as on a loop until a sort of peace can calmly envelop any investigative minds.

The gift to envision all of that, without being contaminated, is like trying to find a needle that perhaps was not meant to be found without becoming an archetype figure or shape-shifter in modern society, which many people go through just to leave those concepts static, sometimes hidden, just to resume them when more wisdom has been found.

The Difference for Unbound People

Half-heart into a light
before the sunset, seeking a whole
from west to east, from south to north.

One lady was wondering
if she left a sign of her presence
in careful paws.

Small marks
to reassure a covenant
for such adventure.

Has she found peace
planning a jump
from the cave of wiser men and women?

The differences being reflected
in an imaginary mirror,
those wonders have found for themselves.

Note: There are people born as complete. Or at least they achieve this mindfulness status which seems a cruel detachment sometimes. Cognitive perception can tell when someone, against one's will, finds herself or himself in such transitory period. So used to refer to a female at first sight because women are more relentless at pushing the limits of knowledge or in discovering themselves in this modern era. Then pointed out that transitory status using the appellative "those" because everyone can find themselves on that strange path which every culture deals with using different knowledge or methods, trying to reach the same decent outcome. Greek philosophers called it the highest good or supreme good.

The Weight of Flower

Confused ideas or ideology
on the edge of millennia that have past,
was enough or it wasn't.

Someone out on the town
seizes a flower.
Has not its weight
made a strong resonance?

Could an excuse be enough
to return what blind eyes
have showed and stolen for a while?

No words will be necessary,
only her permission
before going back to wonder.

Note: In a few relationships, or maybe in just one relationship with a woman, men found themselves as though enchanted, asking to be freed or distanced from certain boundaries. The reason seems obscure sometimes, but there is an instinct of preservation that guides such request; it's not because men don't want those relationships. Actually, they already feel that will not give an outcome where certain values could be built into it.

Obviously, it is clear that those cases happen also for a woman toward a man.

Dancing Woman

Dancer of this life,
struggling with a smile,
blessed hand given to a stranger
that came out his limbo, faded away.

Some memories observe who keeps them far away.
No feeling of envy are able to touch them,
that passion which a woman
usually has to dance with herself.

Any observer acquired that weightless smile
useful in the journey
through the path of life,

where peril is only given
when such a moment is not shared.

The beauty of her youth
and in her aging moment through time,
gifts which one could observe
how every emotion can shape
a face or a body, tasting without approaching.

The Observer views all.
The same light which some eyes possess
is a burden, while even the darkest corner
is revealed for travelling minds,
its purpose should this life give
if not the ability to see, at least once.

Note: The Observer is another way to describe the unconscious mind or the real persona that lives inside each of us. Seems that such a mind comes to life only when responsibility comes into one's life, or when the process of alignment (so called in psychology) comes in essence into a person.

Trying to describe this moment, it is different for everyone regarding the contest in which happens this phenomena. The common pattern is the feeling of affection for someone, or in extreme cases, it could be pain felt for someone else or in itself. In every case, the revealing moment that something has changed is clear in one's life.

The Blossom of a Smile

Collision of souls
that has no planned
outcome or desire.

One remembers a lesson;
the other remembers the teaching,
with no remembrance of the lesson.

So thus a woman be priceless
when a smile can blossom
in her awakening.

Riddle for the Rider

There are lessons
hard to learn,
lessons which life doesn't repeat.

A long travel
begins with one step at the time,
bringing one away from the mist of rusty edge.

A period that never stops
carries on also when we lay asleep.
Can be taken away a teaching
from the glimpse of wet eyes.

Most use the upper chest
to learn the lesson which life's test
comes first, before even we have studied it.

Which lesson is it?
Answer: Knowing one's own breath.

Guidance to the Disguise of One's Emotion

Holding her needs,
Her wrist sighed from
a failed grasp.

Have those who travelled with her
shown comfort,
or has the cup been poisoned
with a raging affair?

So thy enemy of hers
at the end was her own
disguised emotion.

How can a woman aspire
to be what cannot be
without the dictation of time and experience?

Nature, after all,
doesn't let her be a whole
without sacrificing
of its own identity.

Into the Ruin of What Was Taken

Chaos cannot be one more
thing at the time.
Falsehood of mystic power.

Some taste the ruins of some choices,
some learn to rebuild,
others ignore the sign.

There was at the beginning
no acceptance, even if was imposed by nature,
only the sound of bones
hitting a wall.

What has been taken
has been given again, the rediscovery
of how a person should love
someone who doesn't take time
to know the possession of one's own heartbeat.

So sometimes digging in memories
or just listening gives justice to those hearts
that have chosen battle instead of committing.
Who can tell if one is ready?
Only the strong will live one day at a time.
The will, one of few things that remains in the ruin
of what was taken.

The Empty Bench

Empty bench, where rests
the cold season ahead,
caged at least those strings
in a limitless apprehension
of leaving one's mind for him or for her,
out of the reach of enslaved thoughts.

Two minds collide in one's shell.
The reality of some footsteps left in the path
were enough to indicate how to handle
the emptiness revealed inside
life's storm.

What can serve an empty bench
to calm while sitting?
Hunger or anger left in the search
of a spring not contaminated by fears.

Notes: In the age of COVID-19, many have opened their eyes to what and how the virus can change human life through struggle for evolution or at least to test potential. Human relations have changed, taken a step back and reconsidering approaching a conversation or having a summary about how life brought this compliance to everyone's daily routine.

So the empty bench is a metaphor to indicate how a simple wood seat in a middle of a park still helps in facing why such simple spot has been replaced by the fear of emptiness that has enveloped an entire world.

A young man once approached while I was sitting on a bench. As we discussed life, my attention was drawn to how he displayed his feeling towards his family, and yet how he was battling the negative thoughts regarding keeping and preserving those feelings or letting them dissipate.

I noticed that just being a listener relieved the burden of the young man. We were helping each other's knowing, but at the same time without acknowledging such a mental process.

The Oblivion in an Emotion

Living in shadows,
resemblance of ambiguity,
salty water can help to clean up
what the psychic mind cannot.

Game of twisted feelings.
Why, if so much gold has been conquered,
it remains as a rusty picture in decayed or forgotten
hands?

Moving thy body is almost hard
for those who don't feel safe.
The oblivion can be found in an emotion.

What can be looked for
in such a mood of not remembering?
In such a state of oblivion, where empty pages

can be filled with words which are enough
to draw a border from such explanation?

An emotion is not a truth
daring the knowledge from where comes
the daily adventure.
Moulding inside such state—state of oblivion—
can bring or alleviate clarification in one or more lives.

Note: Baring emotions or their identification is not easy to recall when life is lived
in fast manner, although it seems commonplace.

The state of oblivion, or not remembering, give time; it's like a backup for the minds
regarding their internal states and the environments around them. For example, when
a couple argues, one can go out of the normal way to approach a confrontation on
the argued topic. What happens most of the time is that the strong emotion seems
to prevail on a reasonable solution on the matter. Strangely enough, it explains the
state of oblivion which that emotion leaves at its passage after arguing with those
we love or those we do not love.

The Colour of One Love

A garden of memories,
where the writer or the reader ever belongs.
Resume the sovereign in unity
from past love is a delicacy
if taken gently.

From a tropical land
cherished is a soul of woman;
time has changed her aspect and persona,
but even through that, such colour is not forgotten.

A writer should capture such spectrum of light;
words don't help at all.
A lady wearing her glasses
hides a key for those moments.

Hands that kissed each other's,
a conflict between burning lips.
No flame is wasted
if let into a shelter outside the indiscrete viewer.

What an intentional moment
to be lived without being sold out!

Who does not go through
if not into a garden of thorns and lies,
just to perceive the scent of some truthful flowers?

The Individuation of a Purpose

There are two friends,
two ladies with a common purpose,
who have taken what is not visible with a scope.
Left someone with few choices
and a foggy identity.
Haven't they stolen from own plates
a fruit hard to harbour.

Dreadful adventures in others' hearts or minds,
time fades away; the ladies question themselves,
'Is such fruit still possible to recover
from a seed of one individuation?'

The identity of a seed
is similar to a feeling of uncomfortable growing,
certainty, at least rest
with those with whom a roof is shared.

What She Never Needs If not Having, not Longing

A servant walks as many,
empty armour
with a cold will, far from many needs.

Some try to catch
what she never needs.
What is it?
The need to feel a longing emotion.

Was such as
hide behind the curtain of thy reality?
Seen a sister helping her sibling
to look for it?

The armour goes to sleep,
leaving his will

as a blanket for thy wanderer.

What she never needs if not having, not longing.

Note: The noun "servant" is used to describe the affliction or burden to understand that sometimes happens that too much feeling leaves a void, reflecting the status of emptiness. "Cold will" identifies what moves the armour or shell—synonymous with "a body"—beyond the need itself.

Women are more able to understand which need has to be done or left undone. That's also why this is more a composition towards the evaluation on which unconscious and conscious frame how a female values her needs as with or without others' support.

That Heart in Those Hands

Flourish autumn,
with brown leaves, has led a path
for the winter.

No reason to freeze
with amusement of a cold past.
What is she carrying in her hands?

Strange minds are dissolved
when those become warm
during this run for a cosy shelter.

Which choices can be taken
with a heart in thy hands?

The Need for a Moment

Sweet aging through the season.
Awakened for a while, a fox
sets up its nest in to earth's roots.

Who is looking for such a moment?
Has not the sun found its way
between tree's leaves?

Has been their search
for a moment being warmed up

with the understanding of making one's own nest
a warm place for future memories?

The Wind's Strength

Being static, no minds at all,
someone can see through unbound eyes
how nature moves everything.

There is no explanation
if travellers go with no worry.
Wise feelings just warn
of not being more than what is necessary.

The wind's strength
is not a cold prison.
Teach how to breathe deep,
so to release one more beat.

When this element goes with
tower's bell, release comfort
from all worries, a plain sound
common in almost every culture.

Is it beautiful, meeting such an invisible element
with a heartbeat?

Lady

Pleasure is not a search
for a sign of an author or a kiss
without a will in it.

Forbidden two bodies
that look for an agreement,
for which a paint of feeling's communion
can be discovered.

It was desire or its absence
that made desist or fallen apart
such a search.

So real hands could touch
and take over a silent pain
that a body backs up into one's consciousness.

There she stood up
as a friend of herself.
Relief in her black/brown eyes
brings memories shall
that some teaching needs
just someone to be
rediscovered or brought to life once more.

Lullaby for a Woman

Maybe you have pushed
beyond the brink of life,
unbound as many others,
destined to fade with one case.

Promise to a mother or mothers
an exchanged value
to still be there, or here,
or somewhere else
seen with disguised eyes.

A shrine not forgotten.
Do not thy wanderers provoke destiny
that was unveiled in a grateful way
to have met another traveller?

A moment of blue is a gift
to the multitude of themselves.
Resonance of many hearts
collided in one's heart.

What Lies in a Dream

Loving, or at least
caring, for a moment
that still keeps
a world in balance,
where a dream lies.

Running with blue lights,
felt the duty of love
or the love for duty,
can a promise be arrested,
without being gentle.

What are your words
for one's neglect?
A person didn't see any neglected minds, lady,
only a rushing desire
to know a side of you.

The Melody of Those Hearts

What if instead of rushing
into an unknown mind,
some hearts could trust
in the small steps of a gentle stranger.

Let mine hands
take care of your speech.
Let assurance posed delicately
by an old man to an enraged spirit,
show a different way
to live with heavy feelings and mould them into
caring thoughts.

Let mix your beats.
No fear will land on your wish,
where once anyone can be blinded
from the melody of a fast heart.

Note: Some people come in others' lives with no purpose at all. People can complete our way to talk or make more deep resonance in understanding ourselves and others. Not to misunderstand the feeling of attachment that envelops such situations at the beginning and then reach the stages of acceptance and letting go.

Because as many I believe that those were moments made with the intention to give a meaning without transforming all in a stage or a hunt for an unfurnished scenario which the retrospective outcome seems not so clear in the eyes of those more gifted than others.

Where a Feeling Can Be

There are not many victories
in this life
when one can count those moments
if a feeling cannot be left in one place.

What is explored
if one persona doesn't belong
to a conscience or
to hidden eyes?

Where is this feeling,
knowing the sound of release
of described suffering?

Are those feelings still travelling?

Multiform of an Emotion

Praying under a soft rain,
deliverance in blank page
of unwritten story.

Anyone who has known once
the lonely tear for a love or a lover,
can those words describe many
or only the circumstances?

Destiny seems like a wolf,
a hand kept in its mouth.
Such a wild animal will leave or release
the grasp for a word of trust.

Has an emotion changed its own form?
Uncertainty is to not let oneself be shaken
or moved even if one's hand
is given to a nature-sharpened claim.

Seeing how a woman can change
an emotion through a gesture
or with her voice,
without hiding the need to know about
how to define a new reality.

Time reveals a meaning
behind a rushed writing.
Or it is more easily possessed
by a multiform feeling
or keeping one's hands inside a measure
of what can be known.

One's mind or body could be absent
from such needs; maybe it's there
where a woman can mould different emotions.

The Lines of Her Eyes

Can my persona stop for a moment?
Need to observe more closely.
No malicious intention
is just the first real need.

Are those lines that define your eyes
reachable to be touched?
If I could steal them,
maybe she'll drop her guard.
Or maybe she'll leave to a stranger
to conserve them.

It was this, my first need of her.

A Distant Voice

She spoke,
tasting her own assurance
that one wish was never
expressed or declared

so could come to her
outside the grip
of a world
made of what she didn't know.

Her feelings
took a small place
in thy shell.

No need to consume such flame,
or the idea of it
could let her just watch
if what was taught was a real teaching
or not.
So she could learn that emotion
without feeling it.

No pushed needs;
lack of reassurance
on the edge, there is only one balance
or the illusion of it.

Printed in the United States
by Baker & Taylor Publisher Services